CELEBRATION

Rosh HaShanah
and
Yom Kippur

WOMEN'S LEAGUE FOR
CONSERVATIVE JUDAISM

Front Cover: *Torah Mantles for the High Holidays. Phyllis Kantor, 1988. Courtesy of Congregation Brith Sholom, Bethlehem, Pennsylvania. Photograph: Ken White.*

Artwork courtesy of:
The Jewish Museum, New York, NY,
  courtesy of Art Resource, New York, NY
The Library of The Jewish Theological
  Seminary of America, New York, NY
Temple Israel of Great Neck, Great Neck, NY
In the Spirit Gallery, New York, NY

First Edition July 1991
ISBN # 0-936293-04-7

©Women's League for Conservative Judaism
  48 East 74 Street
  New York, New York 10021

Contents

Introduction

■

". . .This is the day the world was called into being; this day all the creatures of the universe stand in judgment before You as children or as servants. . ."

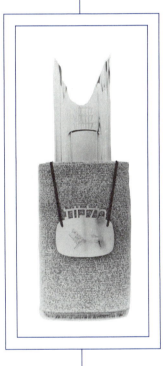

The message of the high holidays is one of serious introspection and spiritual renewal for Jews everywhere. For *Rosh HaShanah*, the birthday of the world, is a time when we are judged anew.

During the *Yamim Nora'im*, the ten day period from the start of *Rosh HaShanah* through the end of *Yom Kippur*, we focus on God's role and His relationship with all His creations. God remembers His covenant with Israel and renews His promise to redeem His people from suffering and oppression. God takes our deeds into account and, with justice and mercy, inscribes us in the Book of Life. Perhaps the most important way we focus on this is through prayer.

Set of Torah Ornaments. Moshe Zabari, 1966. Silver, fabricated, pierced and hammered; gold and leather. The Jewish Museum

"Prayer clarifies our hopes and intentions. It helps us discover our true aspirations, the pangs we ignore, the longings we forget. It is an act of self-purification, a quarantine for the soul. It gives us the opportunity to be honest, to say what we believe, and to stand for what we say."

Rabbi Abraham Joshua Heschel, *Between God and Man*

We break the *Yom Kippur* fast with renewed strength and inspiration, hoping that the new year will be one of good health and blessings for those we cherish, as well as for ourselves.

To help impart the spirit of the high holidays, we joyously present this manual. It is part of the Women's League *CELEBRATION* Series and is a guide to enrich our observance of *Rosh HaShanah* and *Yom Kippur*. We discuss the significance and history of this time, and its special laws, prayers, and customs. We also include a statement about the Jewish calendar at this season, starting with the first day of the Hebrew month of *Elul*, which signals that it is time to prepare for the holy days ahead. Challenging study questions, a list of resource materials, recipes, and a glossary of terms complete the book, which we hope you will enjoy and find useful.

The members of the Publications Committee
are grateful to Women's League President,
Audrey Citak, for the opportunity to work on
this exciting project and for her encourage-
ment. We also appreciate the contributions of
many devoted volunteers who helped to
research and write it, especially: Past National
President, Ruth Perry; Vice-President, Joyce
Goldberg; and Dr. Shelley Buxbaum. Our thanks
to Rabbi Allen Juda and Congregation Brith
Sholom for our cover photograph. Our thanks
also to the Women's League professional staff
for its valuable guidance: Executive Director,
Bernice Balter; Education Director, Edya Arzt;
and special thanks to Public Relations Director,
Rhonda Kahn.

To you, our readers, we wish a year of health
and happiness!

לְשָׁנָה טוֹבָה תִּכָּתֵבוּ

L'shanah Tovah T'katayvu

May you be inscribed for a good year!

Helene Schachter, Chairman
Publications Committee
Women's League for Conservative Judaism

Days of Awe

osh HaShanah and Yom Kippur, the Yamim Nora'im, the "Days of Awe," are holy days, linked with the hopes and aspirations of all mankind— but unlike the Festivals, they are not related to any particular historical event or to any agricultural cycle. Rosh HaShanah, Yom Kippur and the intermediary days are known as the Aseret Y'may T'shuvah, the "Ten Days of Repentance." They acknowledge the beginning of a new year and atonement for misdeeds in the old year, and are characterized by humility, trepidation and dramatic solemnity. The image of each person standing in judgment before God predominates the season, as we reiterate our intention to perform God's will, as well as our desires for moral self-renewal.

Torah Crown. Bezalel School, Jerusalem, 20th century. Silver, hammered, filigree and repousse; turquoise, jade and bone, carved. The Jewish Museum

5

There are three Biblical descriptions of *Rosh HaShanah*. In Leviticus 23:24 we read, "In the seventh month, on the first day of the month, you shall observe complete rest, a sacred

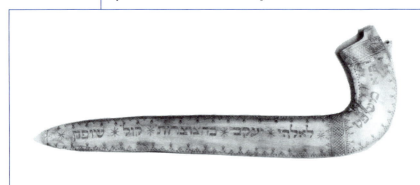

occasion commemorated with loud blasts;" in Numbers 29:1, "In the seventh month, on the first day of the month, you shall observe a sacred occasion: you shall not work at your occupations. You shall observe it as a day when the horn is sounded." The observance of *Rosh HaShanah* is also described in the Book of Nehemiah, chapter 8. On the first day of the seventh month, Ezra the Scribe read from the "Book of the Law" before the people. He enjoined them not to despair, but, rather, to celebrate and rejoice in the Lord.

Rosh HaShanah is known by three different names, each describing a major component of the season: *Yom HaDin*, the Day of Judgment; *Yom HaZikaron*, the Day of Remembrance; and, *Yom T'ruah*, the Day of the Sounding of the *Shofar*. At this time, God the Judge deliberates on the fate of each human being, based on his or her actions of the preceding year.

Yom Kippur, the Day of Atonement, a day of fasting, prayer, and self-evaluation, is the day on which God passes judgment on every living creature. The theme of Divine forgiveness through sincere prayer *(t'fillah)*, repentance *(t'shuvah)*, and living justly *(tz'dakah)* which is woven into both the *Rosh HaShanah* and the *Yom Kippur* liturgy, reflects our sincere desire to reinforce our relationship with God. However, responsibility for reconciliation also extends to relationships between ourselves and those around us. We ask their forgiveness for any wrongdoing, and resolve to improve our relationships.

Cover of Maḥzor. Italy, early 17th century. Silver, engraved and embossed. The Jewish Museum

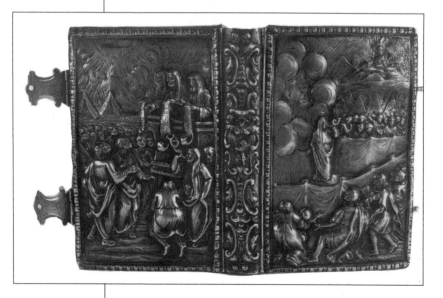

Fragment of Torah Ark. New York, ca. 1900. Wood, carved, gilt and poly-chrome. The Jewish Museum

The observance of *Yom Kippur* has been altered radically in the course of history. In the days of the Temple in Jerusalem, elaborate sacrificial rituals were performed to atone for the sins of the people on the one day when the *Kohen Gadol* (High Priest) pronounced the otherwise unspoken Name of God in the Holy of Holies and sent a symbolic scapegoat into the wilderness. Today, this scene is retold during the synagogue *Avodah* service, since the synagogue ritual has replaced the Temple ritual.

Days of Awe —
Days of Rejoicing

*T*he solemnity of the *Yamim Nora'im* builds up gradually, beginning with *Rosh Ḥodesh Elul*—

the first day of the month before *Rosh HaShanah* —when the *shofar* is blown in the synagogue at the conclusion of the *Shaḥarit* (morning) service. The *shofar* is blown again every morning of *Elul*, except on *Shabbat* when the *shofar* is never sounded. It is not blown on the day before *Rosh HaShanah* to distinguish between the "custom" of blowing the *shofar* during *Elul* and the "commandment" of blowing the *shofar* on *Rosh HaShanah*. These blasts are a reminder that we must begin the process of *t'shuvah*.

Torah Case with finials. Maurice Mayer, Paris, ca. 1860. Silver, repousse, cast, and parcel-gilt. The Jewish Museum

It is customary during this period to visit the graves of parents, relatives and friends to pay respect and to be inspired by their lives. It is also a tradition to make charitable contributions to support synagogues and communal institutions.

On a Saturday evening close to *Rosh HaShanah*, a service known as *S'liḥot* takes place at midnight in the synagogue. This timing is derived from Psalm 119: "At midnight I will rise to give thanks to You because of Your righteous ordinances." This service consists of the recitation of the most moving of the penitential prayers of repentance and forgiveness as well as of selected readings. Several times during the service, we recite the "Thirteen Attributes of God" which are taken from Exodus 34:6-7. The specific penitential prayers, the *S'liḥot*, are also recited on at least four days before *Rosh HaShanah*, often at dawn, to help us further prepare for the days ahead. Jewish mystics believed that God's mercy was pre-eminent during these early hours.

It is during the *S'liḥot* service that the special *nusaḥ*, or liturgical melodies, of the *Yamim Nora'im* is introduced in the synagogue. The High Holidays are characterized by their own distinctive *nusaḥ*, including, as well, special cantillations for the *Torah* and *Haftarah* readings.

The primary observance of *Rosh HaShanah* on the first and second days of the month of *Tishri* is the synagogue service, during which one hears the blasts of the *shofar.*

The *Shabbat* between *Rosh HaShanah* and *Yom Kippur* is of special significance as indicated by its name: *Shabbat Shuvah*—the *Shabbat* of Return. The *Haftarah* for the day is taken from the Prophet Hosea (14:2-10) and opens with the words, "Return *(Shuvah),* O Israel, to the Lord, your God." It further reiterates our need to live in accordance with the laws of God.

Simḥat Torah Flag. Poland, 19th century. Woodcut. The Jewish Museum

Yom Kippur, the tenth day of *Tishri,* is the climax of the *Yamim Nora'im.* Beginning before sunset with the penetrating notes of the *Kol*

Nidre prayer in which we ask that all vows to God be annulled, *Yom Kippur* ends twenty-five hours later, affirming God's greatness on notes of hope and expectation.

Traditionally, it is during the evening after the conclusion of *Yom Kippur* that the first nail is driven into the *sukkah* in preparation for the Festival of *Sukkot,* the Feast of Booths, which comes five days after *Yom Kippur.* It is one of three Pilgrimage Festivals and marks the harvest season and the dwelling in booths of our ancestors during the exodus.

According to some *Midrashim,* it is not until *Hoshana Rabba* (the seventh day of *Sukkot)* that the verdict passed on *Yom Kippur* is finally and irrevocably "sealed." It is believed that until this day, there is yet some recourse regarding the judgment of *Yom Kippur. Shmini Atzeret,* the "Eighth Day of Assembly," introduces a prayer for rain (in the land of Israel). *Simḥat Torah* on 23 *Tishri* marks the communal reading of the last chapter of the *Torah* in the Book of Deuteronomy, followed immediately by the reading of the first chapter of the first book, Genesis. Thus the cycle of the High Holiday season ends with a new beginning.

In The
Synagogue

THE MAḤZOR

The magnitude of the synagogue observance of
the *Yamim Nora'im* is illustrated by the very
length of its liturgy and by the prayer book
devoted exclusively to it. The *Maḥzor* (literally
"cycle") is an anthology of Jewish literature,
including prayers created in the days of the
Temple; selections from the Bible, *Talmud*, and
Midrash; and, in many editions, modern

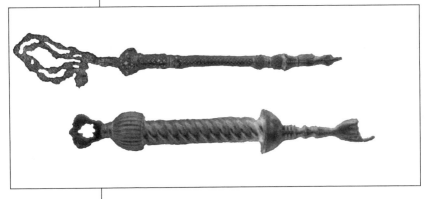

contributions. *Piyyutim*, compositions of the
liturgical poets of the Middle Ages, punctuate
the liturgy.

One of the outstanding prayers, unique to the *Maḥzor*, is the *Hin'ni* ("Here Am I"). In this deeply stirring personal prayer an unknown *ḥazzan* (cantor) humbly presents himself as deficient in good deeds, overwhelmed and awed by the responsibility of representing the congregation before God.

THE SHOFAR

The most prominent feature of the observance of *Rosh HaShanah* or *Yom T'ruah*—the Day of the Blowing of the Horn—is the sounding of the *shofar*. We learn in the *Mishnah* (*Rosh HaShanah* 3:2) that although any horn from a sheep, goat or antelope is acceptable as a *shofar*, a ram's horn is preferable because it recalls the story of the binding of Isaac, for whom a ram was substituted at the last moment. According to Saadia Gaon (882-942), who served as the head of the great Talmudic academies of Sura and Pumbeditha, there are ten reasons for blowing the *shofar*, two of which are specifically related to *Rosh HaShanah:* 1) to proclaim the sovereignty of God on *Rosh HaShanah*, and 2) as a warning to the people to repent for their wrongdoings. Moses Maimonides (1135-1204), writing in his *Mishneh Torah*, says, "All are required to hear the sounding of the *shofar:* Priests, Levites, and Israelites."

Three basic notes are prescribed for the public blowing of the *shofar: t'kiah* (blast), one long clear unbroken note; *sh'varim* (broken), three short blasts; and *t'ruah* (alarm), a quick succession of nine staccato sounds. At the end, an additional note is sounded, *T'kiah G'dolah* (the great blast), one note sustained as long as possible. Many communities encourage the participation of children by inviting each child to blow his *shofar* for the congregation.

Shofar, ram's horn. North Africa or Yemen, 19th century. The Jewish Museum

ROSH HASHANAH SERVICES

As on all *Shabbatot* and Festivals, there are three sections to the morning service for *Rosh HaShanah: Shaharit* (morning service), Torah service with *Haftarah*, and *Musaf* (additional service).

The sounding of the *shofar*, the distinctive feature before and during *Musaf*, punctuates and concludes three of its segments: *Malkhuyot*, *Zikhronot* and *Shofarot. Malkhuyot* (Sovereignty) pronounces the kingship of God over the universe. *Zikhronot* (Remembrance) reminds us of God's role throughout history. Lastly, *Shofarot* (Horns) expresses faith in the future.

The first *Torah* reading for the first day, Genesis 21, tells of the birth of Isaac, which is believed to have occurred on *Rosh HaShanah*. The *Haftarah* from I Samuel (1:1-2:10) recounts Hannah's passionate plea to God for the birth of a son and her hymn of joy when her prayer is answered.

On the second day, we read of the binding of Isaac (Genesis 22), a story of unquestioning faith and obedience to God. The *Haftarah*, from the Prophet Jeremiah (31:2-20), portrays Rachel weeping for her children and God's assurance that they will be restored to the land of their fathers.

The afternoon *Minḥah* and evening *Ma'ariv* services for *Rosh HaShanah* follow the format of every Festival with the addition of *piyyutim*. After the second day, *Ma'ariv* includes *Havdalah*, which may also be recited at home, to distinguish between the holy days and the regular week.

YOM KIPPUR SERVICES

Confession of sins on *Yom Kippur* serves to cleanse the human spirit and is the first step to repentance. The oldest formula of confession said by the High Priest in the Temple is: "I have done wrong, I have transgressed, and I have sinned." The Rabbis of the Gaonic period (700-1100) formalized the recitation of a confession and incorporated it into the liturgy. Thus, on *Yom Kippur* we read the *Al Ḥet* (". . . for the sins") prayer which contains a long list of sins written in the plural to stress communal responsibility. Each worshipper recites the list and "beats" his chest as a symbol of contrition. The *Al Ḥet* is preceded by a shortened confessional, arranged in alphabetical order, beginning with the word *"Ashamnu"* ("We are guilty"). Another confession is the *Avinu Malkaynu* ("Our Father, our King") arranged as a double acrostic, listing forty-four transgressions.

Bible. Germany, 14th century. First Book of Samuel. The Jewish Museum

Yom Kippur is structured around five services, more than are prescribed for any other day.

It begins with the *Kol Nidre* ("All Vows") prayer which must be completed before sundown. A symbolic "court" is convened and the *ḥazzan* chants the legal formula for the annulment of vows three times.

> "By authority of the court on high and by the authority of this court below. . .we hereby declare that it is permitted to pray with those who have transgressed. . .
> All vows and oaths that we have taken, all promises and obligations that we have made to God. . .we hereby publicly retract . . .and declare our intention to be absolved of them."

The remainder of the *Ma'ariv* service includes the standard evening liturgy together with a number of special *piyyutim* and *s'liḥot.*

The morning service, *Shaḥarit,* is similar to that of any Festival with the addition of *piyyutim.* The reading from the first *Torah* (Leviticus 16) describes the ceremonies conducted in the Second Temple in Jerusalem on the Day of Atonement. A reading from a second Torah scroll (Numbers 29:7-11) describes the communal sacrifices for this day.

The *Haftarah* from the Prophet Isaiah (57:14-58:14) deals with the true purpose of fasting: only by the elimination of evil and with righteous conduct can prayer and fasting bring hope and promise.

The *Yizkor* "Memorial" service** usually follows the Torah service.

Musaf includes two special sections, the *Avodah* and the Martyrology. The *Avodah* service is comprised of the vivid Mishnaic description of the prayer, sacrifices and pageantry conducted in the Temple on *Yom Kippur*, while the Martyrology graphically recounts the martyrdom of ten great Jewish leaders during the Roman persecution. In many synagogues today, a portion of the Martyrology is devoted to contemporary readings relating to the Holocaust.

Yahrzeit
"Memorial" Light.
Shirley Kagan,
New York.
Crystal, carved.
In The Spirit
Gallery

The *Minhah* service includes a Torah reading from Leviticus 18, and a *Haftarah* reading of the Book of Jonah which assures us that God's forgiveness is readily extended to those whose *t'shuvah* is sincere.

The fifth and final service of *Yom Kippur* is *N'ilah*, the full name of which is *N'ilat Sh'arim* or the "Closing of the Gates," referring to the daily closing of the Temple gates in ancient times. On *Yom Kippur*, the "gates of heaven," which have remained open to prayer

**Note that there is no halakhic prohibition against remaining in the synagogue during Yizkor, even for those not reciting kaddish.

19

until sunset, are symbolically closed. Worshippers stand throughout the service.

The entire *Yom Kippur* ritual culminates with the congregation reciting the *Shma*, once, followed by three proclamations of "Praised be His glorious sovereignty throughout all time," and seven repetitions of "The Lord, He is God." A single *shofar* blast, a *T'kiah G'dolah*, announces the end of this sacred day. *Ma'ariv*, including *Havdalah*, is then recited.

The N'ilah Closing Ritual

Reader and congregation:

שְׁמַע יִשְׂרָאֵל יְיָ אֱלֹהֵינוּ יְיָ אֶחָד:

Shma Yisrael Adonai Elohaynu Adonai eḥad.
Hear, O Israel: the Lord is our God, the Lord is One.

Reader and congregation, three times:

בָּרוּךְ שֵׁם כְּבוֹד מַלְכוּתוֹ לְעוֹלָם וָעֶד:

Barukh shem k'vod malkhuto l'olam va'ed.
Praised be His glorious sovereignty for ever and ever.

Reader and congregation, seven times:

יְיָ הוּא הָאֱלֹהִים:

Adonai hu HaElohim.
The Lord He is God.

The shofar is sounded.

תְּקִיעָה גְדוֹלָה

T'kiah G'dolah
The great blast.

לְשָׁנָה הַבָּאָה בִּירוּשָׁלָיִם:

L'shanah haba'ah birushala'yim.
Next year in Jerusalem!

Personal Observance

THE *YAMIM NORA'IM*

*T*he traditional greeting on these holy days is לְשָׁנָה טוֹבָה תִּכָּתֵבוּ *"L'shanah tovah t'katayvu"*—"May you be inscribed for a good year" and שָׁנָה טוֹבָה וּמְתוּקָה *"Shanah tovah um'tukah"*—"a good and sweet year." Sephardim add to this, "May you be worthy of abundant years." These New Year greetings are often sent to family and friends in the form of cards which may then be saved to hang as decorations in the *sukkah*.

New Year's Greeting. Attributed to Happy Jack (Eskimo, ca. 1870-1918). Nome, Alaska, 1910. Walrus tusk, engraved, with gold inset. The Jewish Museum

From *Rosh HaShanah* through *Yom Kippur,* as the time of repentance draws to a close, we wish people גְּמַר חֲתִימָה טוֹבָה *"G'mar ḥatimah tovah,"* that they may be "sealed (in the Book of Life) for good," or כְּתִיבָה וַחֲתִימָה טוֹבָה *"K'tivah v'ḥatimah tovah,"* that they may be both "written and sealed (in the Book of Life) for good." On *Yom Kippur,* we add צוֹם קַל *"Tzom kal,"* for a "light or easy fast." It is also customary not to be overly demonstrative in our greetings on *Yom Kippur,* in keeping with the solemnity of the day.

With the exception of *Yom Kippur,* it is a popular tradition to wear new clothing on the holidays to heighten our sense of "new" and "special" and to have additional reasons to recite the *shehecheʼyanu.*

A medieval ceremony that has recently been revived by some Conservative synagogues is that of *Tashlikh*—"and you will cast . . . all your sins into the depths of the sea" (Micah 7:20). On the first afternoon of *Rosh HaShanah,* or on the second if the first is *Shabbat,* people go to a body of water and shake out their pockets or drop bread crumbs into the water. They recite specific prayers indicating that it is in one's own power to "shake off" sins and repent.

ROSH HASHANAH IN THE HOME

The two days of *Rosh HaShanah* are observed with the same prohibition against work as are any Jewish holy days, although one may cook and carry if it is not *Shabbat*. The festival officially begins at sunset on the first of *Tishri* with the lighting of the candles.*

Feasting on *Rosh HaShanah* has its origins in the Book of Nehemiah (8:10) in which the Prophet directs the Children of Israel to "eat of the fat and drink of the sweet." Dinners and lunches with family and friends are among the most sumptuous and festive meals of the Jewish year.

Postcard. Frankfurt a. Main, Germany, 19th century. The Jewish Theological Seminary of America

The special *kiddush** over wine recited before dinner expresses gratitude to God for giving us this *Yom HaZikaron*, this "Day of Remembrance," this *Yom T'ruah*, this "Day of Blowing the

*See page 31ff for this and all other b'rakhot.

Shofar," a holy festival. The *shehehe'yanu**
is added. *Kiddush* is followed by washing the
hands while reciting the *b'rakhah, al n'tilat
yada'yim.**

NEW AND NOVEL
JEWISH POSTAL CARDS

Father and Son

25 DESIGNS—25 CENTS
BLOCH PUBLISHING CO.
738 Broadway   NEW YORK

*Postcard. New
York, NY, 1906.
The Jewish
Theological
Seminary of
America*

The *motzi** (the
b'rakhah over bread) is
said over two *hallot.*
The salt that is usually
sprinkled on *hallah* is
replaced with honey for
a sweet new year. Most
often the *hallot* are
round, symbolizing the
roundness of life, God's
crown, a complete
year, or the unending
character of life. They
are sometimes baked in
the shape of a ladder,
or with a ladder across
the top, to indicate that
on *Rosh HaShanah* it is decided "who shall be
exalted and who shall be brought low." Many
bakers add raisins to their New Year *hallot.*

The ceremony which follows further illustrates
the hope that the year ahead will be sweet. We
dip apples or other fruit in honey, and recite
the phrase, "May it be Your will to renew for us
a year that is good and sweet."* On the second

*See page 31ff for this and all other b'rakhot.

26

day, a new fruit is introduced so that the *shehehe'yanu** may again be recited. In some homes, a new fruit is also introduced on the first night. Often a pomegranate is chosen because its many seeds connote fruitfulness and fertility.

Honey Dish.
S. Kagan/I. Puski,
New York.
Porcelain,
painted. In The
Spirit Gallery

The meal, as with all meals in a Jewish home, concludes with the recitation of *birkat hamazon*** which expresses our gratitude to God for the food which we have just eaten, with the specific additions for the festival, and for *Shabbat* when appropriate.

*See page 31ff for this and all other b'rakhot.
**See a complete siddur or mahzor for the birkat hamazon.

YOM KIPPUR IN THE HOME

On *Yom Kippur,* also known as *Shabbat Shabbaton*—the "Sabbath of Sabbaths," all the prohibitions of *Shabbat* (such as cooking) pertain.

However, if *Yom Kippur* falls on a *Shabbat,* it is the only *Shabbat* on which Jews fast. *Yom Kippur* begins before, and ends after, sundown, as do all the days of the Jewish year. Prior to attending the *Kol Nidre* service, the meal is eaten, although candles are not yet lit and *kiddush* is not recited. Care is taken to eat comparatively bland under-seasoned foods, and to drink ample liquid. We are told in the *Talmud* that it is a *mitzvah* to eat and drink well before the fast.

It is customary to light a memorial *(Yahrzeit)* candle which burns throughout *Yom Kippur*

Tz'dakah Box. Hungary, 1860. Silver, engraved, with wooden handle. The Jewish Museum

commemorating members of the family who have died in years past. Before departing for the synagogue, the holiday candles are lit* and parents bless their children as is done on *Shabbat*.*

We observe a 25-hour total fast** on this *Yom HaDin*, this Day of Judgment, in accordance with the Biblical injunction, "and you shall practice self-denial" (Leviticus 16:29). Our rabbis define this as: no food, no drink, no anointing the body, no wearing of leather, and no sexual relations. Some people choose to wear plain white clothing or a *kittel* (white robe) to show purity and an equality of all before the Divine Judge.

At the end of *Yom Kippur*, following the *N'ilah* service, the final *T'kiah G'dolah*, and the evening service, we break the fast. Usually, a dairy meal consisting of juice, breads, cheeses, fish, and sweet desserts is served. Obviously, all shopping and preparations for this meal have been completed prior to the onset of the holiday. Many synagogues provide a collation so that congregants may break the fast together.

---

*See page 31ff for this and all other b'rakhot.

**Fasting should not endanger one's health. The mitzvah of pikuaḥ nefesh (concern for one's physical well-being) takes precedence over fasting. People taking medications regularly, as well as pregnant and nursing women, should consult their physicians. Children below the age of bar/bat mitzvah are not required to fast, although children can be encouraged to avoid eating between meals, or, depending on their age, to skip either breakfast or lunch. The Mishnah says we should train them to fast.

B'rakhot

Rosh HaShanah: Evening

B'RAKHOT OVER FESTIVAL CANDLES

בָּרוּךְ אַתָּה יהוה אֱלֹהֵינוּ מֶלֶךְ הָעוֹלָם, אֲשֶׁר קִדְּשָׁנוּ בְּמִצְוֹתָיו
וְצִוָּנוּ לְהַדְלִיק נֵר שֶׁל (שַׁבָּת וְשֶׁל) יוֹם טוֹב.

*Barukh Atah Adonai Elohaynu Melekh ha'olam asher kid'shanu
b'mitzvotav v'tzivanu l'hadlik ner shel (Shabbat v'. . .*) yom tov.*

Praised are You, Lord our God, King of the universe, for You have
made us holy through Your commandments by bidding us light
the candles of (Shabbat and*) Festivals.

בָּרוּךְ אַתָּה יהוה אֱלֹהֵינוּ מֶלֶךְ הָעוֹלָם, שֶׁהֶחֱיָנוּ וְקִיְּמָנוּ וְהִגִּיעָנוּ
לַזְּמַן הַזֶּה.

*Barukh Atah Adonai Elohaynu Melekh ha'olam shehehe'yanu
v'kiy'manu v'higiyanu laz'man hazeh.*

Praised are You, Lord our God, King of the universe, Who has
kept us in life, sustained us, and enabled us to reach this time.

*When holiday coincides with Shabbat.

KIDDUSH

On Friday night, begin here:

וַיְהִי עֶרֶב וַיְהִי בֹקֶר
יוֹם הַשִּׁשִּׁי. וַיְכֻלּוּ הַשָּׁמַיִם וְהָאָרֶץ וְכָל־צְבָאָם. וַיְכַל אֱלֹהִים
בַּיּוֹם הַשְּׁבִיעִי מְלַאכְתּוֹ אֲשֶׁר עָשָׂה, וַיִּשְׁבֹּת בַּיּוֹם הַשְּׁבִיעִי
מִכָּל־מְלַאכְתּוֹ אֲשֶׁר עָשָׂה. וַיְבָרֶךְ אֱלֹהִים אֶת־יוֹם הַשְּׁבִיעִי
וַיְקַדֵּשׁ אֹתוֹ, כִּי בוֹ שָׁבַת מִכָּל־מְלַאכְתּוֹ אֲשֶׁר בָּרָא אֱלֹהִים
לַעֲשׂוֹת.

Vay'he erev, vay'he voker, yom hashishi.

Vay'khulu hashamay'im v'ha'aretz, v'khol tz'va'am. Vay'khal Elohim bayom hash'vi'i, m'lakhto asher asah, vay'shbot bayom hash'vi'i, mikol m'lakhto asher asah.

Vay'varekh Elohim et yom hash'vi'i vay'kadesh oto, ke vo shavat mikol m'lakh'to asher bara Elohim la'a'sot.

And there was evening and there was morning—

the sixth day. The heavens and the earth, and all they contain, were completed. On the seventh day God completed the work which He had been doing; He ceased on the seventh day from all the work which He had done. Then God blessed the seventh day and called it holy, because on it He ceased from all His work of Creation.

(continued)

סַבְרִי מָרָנָן

בָּרוּךְ אַתָּה יהוה אֱלֹהֵינוּ מֶלֶךְ הָעוֹלָם, בּוֹרֵא פְּרִי הַגֶּפֶן.
בָּרוּךְ אַתָּה יהוה אֱלֹהֵינוּ מֶלֶךְ הָעוֹלָם, אֲשֶׁר בָּחַר בָּנוּ מִכָּל־עָם
וְרוֹמְמָנוּ מִכָּל־לָשׁוֹן, וְקִדְּשָׁנוּ בְּמִצְוֹתָיו. וַתִּתֶּן לָנוּ יהוה אֱלֹהֵינוּ
בְּאַהֲבָה אֶת־יוֹם (הַשַּׁבָּת הַזֶּה וְאֶת־יוֹם) הַזִּכָּרוֹן הַזֶּה, יוֹם
(זִכְרוֹן) תְּרוּעָה (בְּאַהֲבָה) מִקְרָא קֹדֶשׁ, זֵכֶר לִיצִיאַת מִצְרָיִם. כִּי
בָנוּ בָחַרְתָּ וְאוֹתָנוּ קִדַּשְׁתָּ מִכָּל־הָעַמִּים, וּדְבָרְךָ אֱמֶת וְקַיָּם
לָעַד. בָּרוּךְ אַתָּה יהוה מֶלֶךְ עַל כָּל־הָאָרֶץ מְקַדֵּשׁ (הַשַּׁבָּת וְ)
יִשְׂרָאֵל וְיוֹם הַזִּכָּרוֹן.

*Savri m'ranan. Barukh Atah Adonai Elohaynu Melekh ha'olam,
boray p'ri hagafen.*

*Barukh Atah Adonai Elohaynu Melekh ha'olam, asher baḥar
banu mikol am v'rom'manu mikol lashon, v'kid'shanu
b'mitzvotav. Vatiten lanu Adonai Elohaynu b'ahava et yom
(haShabbat hazeh v'et yom*) hizakaron hazeh, yom (zikh'ron*)
t'ruah (b'ahavah*) m'krah kodesh, zekher l'tzi'yat m'tzra'yim. Ke
vanu vaḥarta v'otanu kidashta mikol ha'amim, ud'varkha emet
v'kayam la'ad. Barukh Atah Adonai Melekh al kol ha'aretz
m'kadesh (haShabbat v'*) Yisrael v'yom hazikaron.*

Praised are You, Lord our God, King of the universe, Who creates
fruit of the vine.

Praised are You, Lord our God, King of the universe, Who has
chosen and distinguished us from among all others by adding
holiness to our lives with His *mitzvot*. Lovingly have You given
us the gift of (this Shabbat and*) this Day of Remembrance, a day
for (recalling*) the *shofar* sound, a day for sacred assembly re-
calling the Exodus from Egypt. Thus You have chosen us, endow-
ing us with holiness from among all peoples. Your faithful word
endures forever. Praised are You, King of all the earth, Who hallows
(Shabbat*) the people Israel and the Day of Remembrance.

*When holiday coincides with Shabbat. (continued)

33

On Saturday night add:

בָּרוּךְ אַתָּה יהוה אֱלֹהֵינוּ מֶלֶךְ הָעוֹלָם, בּוֹרֵא מְאוֹרֵי הָאֵשׁ.
בָּרוּךְ אַתָּה יהוה אֱלֹהֵינוּ מֶלֶךְ הָעוֹלָם, הַמַּבְדִּיל בֵּין קֹדֶשׁ לְחֹל
בֵּין אוֹר לְחֹשֶׁךְ, בֵּין יִשְׂרָאֵל לָעַמִּים, בֵּין יוֹם הַשְּׁבִיעִי לְשֵׁשֶׁת
יְמֵי הַמַּעֲשֶׂה. בֵּין קְדֻשַּׁת שַׁבָּת לִקְדֻשַּׁת יוֹם טוֹב הִבְדַּלְתָּ, וְאֶת־
יוֹם הַשְּׁבִיעִי מִשֵּׁשֶׁת יְמֵי הַמַּעֲשֶׂה קִדַּשְׁתָּ, הִבְדַּלְתָּ וְקִדַּשְׁתָּ אֶת־
עַמְּךָ יִשְׂרָאֵל בִּקְדֻשָּׁתֶךָ. בָּרוּךְ אַתָּה יהוה הַמַּבְדִּיל בֵּין קֹדֶשׁ
לְקֹדֶשׁ.

Barukh Atah Adonai Elohaynu Melekh ha'olam, boray m'oray ha'esh.

*Barukh Atah Adonai, Elohaynu Melekh ha'olam, hamavdil bayn kodesh
l'khol, bayn ohr l'hoshekh, bayn yisrael la'amim, bayn yom hash'vi'i
l'shayshet y'may hama'a'seh. Bayn k'dushat Shabbat lik'dushat yom tov
hiv'dalta, v'et yom hash'vi'i, mishayshet y'may hama'aseh kidashta,
hiv'dalta v'kidashta et a'mkha yisrael b'k'dushatekha. Barukh Atah Adonai,
hamavdil bayn kodesh l'kodesh.*

Praised are You, Lord our God, King of the universe Who creates the lights
of fire.

Praised are You, Lord our God, King of the universe Who has endowed all
creation with distinctive qualities, distinguishing between sacred and secular
time, between light and darkness, between the people Israel and other
peoples, between the seventh day and the six working days of the week.
You have made a distinction between the sanctity of Shabbat and the sanctity
of Festivals, and have hallowed Shabbat more than the other days of the
week. You have set Your people Israel apart, making their lives holy through
attachment to Your holiness. Praised are You, Lord Who distinguishes one
sacred time from another.

(continued)

בָּרוּךְ אַתָּה יהוה אֱלֹהֵינוּ מֶלֶךְ הָעוֹלָם שֶׁהֶחֱיָנוּ וְקִיְּמָנוּ וְהִגִּיעָנוּ לַזְּמַן הַזֶּה.

Barukh Atah Adonai Elohaynu Melekh ha'olam shehehe'yanu v'kiy'manu v'higiyanu laz'man hazeh.

Praised are You, Lord our God, King of the Universe, Who has kept us in life, sustained us and enabled us to reach this time.

B'RAKHAH AFTER WASHING HANDS

בָּרוּךְ אַתָּה יהוה אֱלֹהֵינוּ מֶלֶךְ הָעוֹלָם, אֲשֶׁר קִדְּשָׁנוּ בְּמִצְוֹתָיו וְצִוָּנוּ עַל נְטִילַת יָדָיִם.

Barukh Atah Adonai Elohaynu Melekh ha'olam asher kid'shanu b'mitzvotav, v'tzivanu al netilat yada'yim.

Praised are You, Lord our God, King of the Universe, for You have made us holy through Your commandments by bidding us rinse our hands.

MOTZI AND EATING ḤALLAH

בָּרוּךְ אַתָּה יהוה אֱלֹהֵינוּ מֶלֶךְ הָעוֹלָם, הַמּוֹצִיא לֶחֶם מִן הָאָרֶץ.

Barukh Atah Adonai Elohaynu Melekh ha'olam hamotzi leḥem min ha'aretz.

Praised are You, Lord our God, King of the Universe, Who brings forth bread from the earth.

RECITE BEFORE EATING FRUIT DIPPED IN HONEY

יְהִי רָצוֹן מִלְּפָנֶיךָ יהוה אֱלֹהֵינוּ וֵאלֹהֵי אֲבוֹתֵינוּ שֶׁתְּחַדֵּשׁ עָלֵינוּ שָׁנָה טוֹבָה וּמְתוּקָה.

Yehi ratzon mil'fanekha Adonai Elohaynu Vay'lohay avotaynu shet'ḥadaysh alaynu shanah tovah umetukah.

May it be Your will, Lord our God and God of our fathers, that You renew for us a good and sweet year.

Rosh HaShanah: Day

KIDDUSH

On *Shabbat* begin here:

וְשָׁמְרוּ בְנֵי יִשְׂרָאֵל אֶת־הַשַּׁבָּת, לַעֲשׂוֹת אֶת־הַשַּׁבָּת לְדֹרֹתָם,
בְּרִית עוֹלָם. בֵּינִי וּבֵין בְּנֵי יִשְׂרָאֵל אוֹת הִיא לְעוֹלָם, כִּי שֵׁשֶׁת
יָמִים עָשָׂה יהוה אֶת־הַשָּׁמַיִם וְאֶת־הָאָרֶץ, וּבַיּוֹם
הַשְּׁבִיעִי שָׁבַת וַיִּנָּפַשׁ.

*V'sham'ru b'nai yisrael et haShabbat la'asot et haShabbat l'dorotam b'rit
olam. Bayni u'vayn b'nai yisrael ot he l'olam, ke shayshet yamim asah
Adonai et hashamayim v'et ha'aretz, u'vayom hash'vi'i shavat vayinafash.*

The people Israel shall observe Shabbat, to maintain it as an everlasting
covenant through all generations. It is a sign between Me and the people
Israel for all time, that in six days the Lord made the heavens and the earth,
and on the seventh day He ceased from work and rested.

תִּקְעוּ בַחֹדֶשׁ שׁוֹפָר בַּכֶּסֶה לְיוֹם חַגֵּנוּ.
כִּי חֹק לְיִשְׂרָאֵל הוּא מִשְׁפָּט לֵאלֹהֵי יַעֲקֹב.

*Tik'u vaḥodesh shofar bakeseh l'yom ḥagaynu, ke ḥok l'yisrael
hu m'shpat Lay'lohay Ya'akov.*

Sound the *shofar* on the new moon, announcing our solemn
festival. It is Israel's law and ritual; the God of Jacob calls us
to judgment.

סַבְרִי מָרָנָן
בָּרוּךְ אַתָּה יהוה אֱלֹהֵינוּ מֶלֶךְ הָעוֹלָם, בּוֹרֵא פְּרִי הַגָּפֶן.

*Savri m'ranan. Barukh Atah Adonai Elohaynu Melekh ha'olam,
boray p'ri hagafen.*

Praised are You, Lord our God, King of the universe Who creates
fruit of the vine.

37

B'RAKHAH AFTER WASHING HANDS

בָּרוּךְ אַתָּה יהוה אֱלֹהֵינוּ מֶלֶךְ הָעוֹלָם, אֲשֶׁר קִדְּשָׁנוּ בְּמִצְוֹתָיו
וְצִוָּנוּ עַל נְטִילַת יָדֵיִם.

*Barukh Atah Adonai Elohaynu Melekh ha'olam asher kid'shanu
b'mitzvotav, v'tzivanu al netilat yada'yim.*

Praised are You, Lord our God, King of the Universe, for You have
made us holy through Your commandments by bidding us rinse
our hands.

MOTZI AND EATING ḤALLAH

בָּרוּךְ אַתָּה יהוה אֱלֹהֵינוּ מֶלֶךְ הָעוֹלָם, הַמּוֹצִיא לֶחֶם מִן
הָאָרֶץ.

*Barukh Atah Adonai Elohaynu Melekh ha'olam hamotzi leḥem
min ha'aretz.*

Praised are You, Lord our God, King of the Universe, Who brings
forth bread from the earth.

RECITE BEFORE EATING FRUIT DIPPED IN HONEY

יְהִי רָצוֹן מִלְּפָנֶיךָ יהוה אֱלֹהֵינוּ וֵאלֹהֵי אֲבוֹתֵינוּ שֶׁתְּחַדֵּשׁ עָלֵינוּ
שָׁנָה טוֹבָה וּמְתוּקָה.

*Yehi ratzon mil'fanekha Adonai Elohaynu Vay'lohay avotaynu
shet'ḥadaysh alaynu shanah tovah umetukah.*

May it be Your will, Lord our God and God of our fathers, that
You renew for us a good and sweet year.

38

Before Yom Kippur

B'RAKHOT OVER CANDLES

בָּרוּךְ אַתָּה יהוה אֱלֹהֵינוּ מֶלֶךְ הָעוֹלָם, אֲשֶׁר קִדְּשָׁנוּ בְּמִצְוֹתָיו
וְצִוָּנוּ לְהַדְלִיק נֵר שֶׁל (שַׁבָּת וְשֶׁל*) יוֹם הַכִּפּוּרִים.

Barukh Atah Adonai Elohaynu Melekh ha'olam asher kid'shanu b'mitzvotav v'tzivanu l'hadlik ner shel (Shabbat v'shel*) Yom haKippurim.

Praised are You, Lord our God, King of the universe, for You have made us holy through Your commandments by bidding us light the candles of (Shabbat and*) Yom Kippur.

בָּרוּךְ אַתָּה יהוה אֱלֹהֵינוּ מֶלֶךְ הָעוֹלָם שֶׁהֶחֱיָנוּ וְקִיְּמָנוּ וְהִגִּיעָנוּ
לַזְּמַן הַזֶּה.

Barukh Atah Adonai Elohaynu Melekh ha'olam shehehe'yanu v'kiy'manu v'higiyanu laz'man hazeh.

Praised are You, Lord our God, King of the universe, Who has kept us in life, sustained us, and enabled us to reach this time.

*When holiday coincides with Shabbat.

BLESSING THE CHILDREN

It is customary for parents to place hands on the heads of children being blessed.

For sons:

יְשִׂימְךָ אֱלֹהִים כְּאֶפְרַיִם וְכִמְנַשֶּׁה.

Y'simkha Elohim k'Efrayim v'kh'Minashe.

May God give you the blessings of Ephraim and Menasseh.

For daughters:

יְשִׂימֵךְ אֱלֹהִים כְּשָׂרָה רִבְקָה רָחֵל וְלֵאָה.

Y'simaykh Elohim k'Sarah, Rivka, Raḥel v'Leah.

May God give you the blessings of Sarah, Rebekah, Rachel, and Leah.

Continue for all:

יְבָרֶכְךָ יהוה וְיִשְׁמְרֶךָ. יָאֵר יהוה פָּנָיו אֵלֶיךָ וִיחֻנֶּךָ. יִשָּׂא יהוה
פָּנָיו אֵלֶיךָ, וְיָשֵׂם לְךָ שָׁלוֹם.

Y'vare'kh'kha Adonai v'yishm'rekha. Ya'er Adonai panav elekha vi'ḥune'kha. Yisa Adonai panav elekha v'yasem lekha shalom.

May the Lord bless you and guard you. May the Lord show you favor and be gracious to you. May the Lord show you kindness and grant you peace.

40

Children

*I*t is important to make plans for the entire family to prepare for the high holiday season. There are several activities that offer an opportunity to involve children.

Tz'dakah is a primary component of the *Yamim Nora'im*. Children could set aside a portion of their own allowances during the month of *Elul* to donate to an organization or institution with which they are familiar, or which they have studied. Similarly, clothing and canned or packaged food might be set aside for community drives.

Most synagogues provide age-appropriate services and child care for at least a portion of each day. Parents can thereby spend as much time as possible in the synagogue and children can feel that they, too, have participated in the

לשנה טובה תכתבו
Glückliches Neujahr!

יישמך אלקים כאפרים וכמנשה
בשרה רבקה רחל ולאה

Postcard. Germany (?), 1905. The Jewish Theological Seminary of America

41

day's observance. Parents should familiarize themselves with the services that are available and make the necessary arrangements in advance.

Parents should talk to their children about the history and traditions of the holy days, as well as about what will occur during services. See the bibliography for suggested readings.

Holiday Fare—
Favorite Recipes

O
n *Rosh HaShanah* and before *Yom Kippur,* we traditionally eat meat meals. The break fast menu after *Yom Kippur* is generally a light dairy menu. It is important to drink plenty of fluids both before and after the fast.

We offer sample menus and a few recipes for each of the holiday meals, and suggest you add your favorites.

Rosh HaShanah

MENU 1

Wine for *Kiddush*
*Yom Tov Hallah
Fresh Fruit
*Herbed Squash Soup
*Brisket
Green Vegetable Salad
*Prune and Sweet Potato
  Tzimmes
Rice
*Apple Crisp

MENU 2

Wine for *Kiddush*
*Yom Tov Hallah
Fresh Fruit
*Gefilte Fish Ring
*Carrot Soup
Roast Veal
Green Vegetable Salad
Pareve Noodle Pudding
*Taiglach

*recipe included

43

Hallah

1 package active dry yeast	3 egg yolks
¼ cup warm water (110°)	3 egg whites plus enough water to equal 1 cup
1 tsp. sugar	¼ cup raisins
4½–5½ cups flour	1 egg yolk plus 2 tsp. water for egg wash
2 tsp. salt	(optional)
2 Tbsp. vegetable oil	
¼ cup honey	

Dissolve yeast and sugar in water. Let stand until it looks puffy. In large bowl, mix all other ingredients except raisins and egg wash. Add yeast mixture and mix thoroughly.

Turn onto a lightly floured board and knead 10 minutes. If using mixmaster with a dough hook, knead on low setting approximately 5 minutes. Dough should look smooth and shiny.

Grease a clean straight-sided bowl. Place dough in bowl and turn dough upside-down, so top is greased. Cover with a towel and place in a warm, draft-free place until doubled in bulk. Punch dough down. (May be done to this point, wrapped and refrigerated for 2 days.)

Add raisins to dough and divide into 2 equal parts. Shape into holiday shapes—round, ladder, bird. Cover and let rise until doubled in bulk. Brush tops of breads lightly with egg wash.

Place in preheated 375° oven and bake 25–30 minutes. Cool on rack.

Gefilte Fish Ring

12 large pieces gefilte fish (fresh, from a jar, or can)
2 cups borscht with beets

2 3 oz. pkg. lemon gelatin
3 oz. red horseradish
2 Tbsp. lemon juice

Place gefilte fish pieces around the bottom of a very lightly oiled 4 cup ring mold.

Set aside beets. Bring borscht to a boil. Dissolve gelatin in it. Add horseradish, beets and lemon juice. Cool slightly and add to gefilte fish. Refrigerate several hours or overnight. Unmold and serve.

12 servings

Hallah Board and Knife. Shirley Kagan, New York. Wood, painted. In The Spirit Gallery

Herbed Squash Bisque

3 Tbsp. margarine
1 butternut squash, peeled, seeded, cut into 1" pieces
2 tart green apples, peeled, cored and cut into 1" pieces
1 large onion, peeled, and thinly sliced
1" or 1½" piece ginger, peeled and finely chopped

¾ tsp. fresh rosemary leaves, or ¼ tsp. dried
1 tsp. fresh marjoram leaves, or ¼ tsp. dried
¾ tsp. fresh thyme leaves, or ¼ tsp. dried
4½–5 cups chicken stock
1½–¾ tsp. Kosher salt
Freshly ground black pepper

In large pot, melt margarine. Add squash, apples, onion and ginger. Cover with wax paper. Heat over low heat until vegetables are softened—about 8–10 minutes.

Remove wax paper. Pour in chicken stock, add salt and pepper. Simmer for about 25 minutes until vegetables are cooked.

Puree in food processor or blender. Reheat, adjust seasonings.

10 servings

Carrot Soup

½ cup vegetable oil
1 small onion, sliced
2 medium potatoes, peeled, and cut in small cubes
1 celery stalk, sliced
1 lb. carrots, peeled and sliced
7 cups hot water

4 envelopes G. Washington Golden Seasoning Broth
2 parsley sprigs
1 tsp. salt
½ tsp. pepper
1 Tbsp. potato flour, if necessary
2 tsp. Worcestershire sauce—may use more

In large pot, heat oil.

Add onion, potatoes, celery, carrots. Cook over low heat until celery and onions have wilted. Do not allow them to brown.

Add water, seasoning broth, parsley, salt, and pepper. Bring to a boil, cover, and simmer ½ hour.

Remove parsley.

Blend in blender. Return to pot. Add potato flour, if it is too thin. Add Worcestershire Sauce. Heat and serve.

10 servings

Brisket

3 medium onions,
  peeled and sliced
½ cup water
1 first cut beef brisket,
  about 4 lbs.
2 oz. tomato paste
8 oz. tomato sauce
salt and pepper
3–4 marrow bones
2–3 carrots, peeled
  and sliced into 1"
  pieces

Place water and onions in bottom of large pot. Lay brisket on top. Put tomato paste, tomato sauce, salt and pepper, marrow bones and carrots on top of meat.

Cover and simmer until done—about 2 hours. You may have to add water during cooking. Remove meat, cool slightly, wrap in foil and refrigerate.

Remove marrow from bones and discard bones. Put marrow and all other ingredients from pot into a Foley food mill or press through a strainer. Refrigerate until cold (overnight, if possible). Remove layer of hard fat.

Pour small amount of sauce into bottom of baking pan. Slice meat and place in pan. Pour balance of sauce over all. Heat thoroughly and serve.

8 servings

Prune and Sweet Potato Tzimmes

3 lbs. sweet potatoes
1 lb. prunes, pitted
2 fat meat bones
½ tsp. salt
6–8 Tbsp. honey

½ cup dark brown
 sugar
Juice of ½ of 1 lemon
 to taste

Peel sweet potatoes and cut into large chunks.

Place all ingredients in pot and cover with cold water. Cover and bring to a boil. Simmer for about 2 hours, adding water if necessary.

There should be about ½ cup juice left. Season to taste. Should be slightly tart. Remove meat bones before serving.

8 servings

Plate for Rosh HaShanah. Delft, ca. 1900. Faience. The Jewish Museum

49

Noodle Pudding — Pareve

12 oz. broad noodles
4 large eggs, well beaten
1 tsp. salt
1 20 oz. <u>can</u> crushed pineapple, un-sweetened, drained
4 Tbsp. pareve margarine, melted

¾–1 cup sliced apricots, canned or fresh
1 cup slivered almonds
1 Tbsp. cinnamon mixed with 3 Tbsp. sugar, or to taste

Preheat oven to 375° (350° for glass pan). Grease a 9" × 13" baking dish.

Cook noodles al dente. Drain.

Combine eggs, salt, pineapple, margarine and apricots. Add noodles.

Pour into baking dish. Sprinkle with almonds and cinnamon-sugar mixture.

Bake, uncovered, 35 minutes.

12 servings

Apple Crisp

½ cup oil
1 cup sugar
2 eggs, lightly beaten
1 tsp. vanilla
1 cup flour
1 tsp. baking powder

3–4 medium apples, peeled and cut into eighths
1 tsp. cinnamon
1 Tbsp. sugar

Preheat oven to 350° (325° for glass pan). Grease and flour 9" or 10" pie plate. Mix together oil and sugar. Add eggs and vanilla. Mix together flour and baking powder. Add to oil mixture and mix well.

Pour batter into pie plate. Place apples on top of batter.

Combine cinnamon and sugar. Sprinkle on top of apples. Bake 50–60 minutes.

8 servings

Taiglach

6 eggs	2 cups sugar
3 Tbsp. vegetable oil	4 cups water
1 tsp. plus 1 Tbsp.	1 cup nuts, coarsely
powdered ginger	chopped (hazelnuts
4 cups flour	or walnuts)
2 cups honey	

Beat eggs. Add oil, 1 tsp. ginger and blend in flour. Knead to form dough.

Roll into strips about ¾" wide. Cut strips into 1" pieces. Set aside on a lightly floured board.

Prepare syrup. Boil honey, sugar and water in large pot. When mixture comes to a rolling boil, drop taiglach into the syrup, a few at a time. When taiglach rise to top, repeat process until all dough is used. Add nuts and stir.

When taiglach are brown and dry (taste), add just a little boiling water and stir well. Add 1 Tbsp. ginger and stir again.

Pour into wide-mouthed jars.

Pre-Yom Kippur Menu

*Yom Tov Ḥallah

Melon

Chicken Soup

*Herbed Chicken

Green Vegetable

Salad

*Carrot Tzimmes

Roasted potatoes

*Plum Torte

*Honey Cake

recipe included

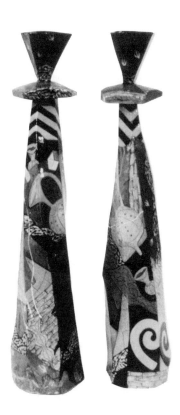

*Candlesticks.
Robert Lipnick,
1990. Ceramic. In
The Spirit Gallery*

Herbed Chicken

2 broiling chickens,
cut into quarters
flour for dredging,
about 1½ cups
salt and pepper
2 tsp. + 2 tsp.
chopped fresh
tarragon
2 tsp. + 2 tsp.
chopped fresh
parsley

2 tsp. + 2 tsp.
chopped fresh
chives
½ lemon
½ cup pareve
shortening
¼ cup lemon juice
½ cup sherry

Preheat oven to 350°. Grease shallow baking dish. Combine flour, salt, pepper and 2 tsp. each of tarragon, parsley and chives in a paper bag. Add 2 pieces of chicken at a time and shake to coat.

Place chicken, skin side down, in baking dish. Sprinkle with the juice of ½ lemon and cover with aluminum foil. Place in oven.

Combine shortening, lemon juice and sherry in a saucepan and heat until shortening is melted.

Baste chicken every 20 minutes for 1–1½ hours or until done. Remove foil. Turn chicken, skin side up, increase oven heat to 400° to let chicken brown. If necessary, add a little more wine or water to the pan.

Sprinkle chicken with remaining chopped fresh herbs.

8 servings

Carrot Tzimmes

4 lbs. carrots, fresh or
 frozen
2 eggs
1 tsp. baking powder
½ cup flour
¼ tsp. salt

2 Tbsp. melted
 pareve margarine
¼ cup (combined)
 dark brown and
 white sugar

Microwave or steam carrots until tender. Preheat oven to 350° (325° for glass pan). Lightly grease 2 quart casserole. Mash carrots and beat thoroughly with eggs. Add remaining ingredients. Pour into casserole. Cover and bake 50 minutes. Remove cover and bake approximately 10 more minutes until firm.

10 servings

Plum Torte

½ cup unsalted
  pareve margarine
⅔ cup sugar
1 cup flour
1 tsp. baking powder
Pinch of salt
2 eggs
½ tsp. vanilla

12 Italian purple plums

Topping:
½ cup light brown
  sugar
½ cup chopped
  walnuts or pecans
1 tsp. (or more)
  cinnamon

Preheat oven to 350°. Grease an 8" or 9" spring-form pan.

Cream sugar and margarine in a bowl. Add flour, baking powder, salt, eggs and vanilla. Beat well.

Halve and pit plums.

Spoon batter into prepared pan. Place plum halves, skin side up, on top of batter.

Combine topping ingredients: sugar, nuts and cinnamon. Sprinkle over plums.

Bake one hour. Cool in pan on rack.

May be frozen. Defrost, then reheat at 300° for 15 minutes. Or defrost in microwave.

8 servings

One Bowl Honey Cake

1 cup sugar
3 cups sifted flour
1½ tsp. baking
  powder
1½ tsp. baking soda
1 tsp. salt
1 tsp. cinnamon
1 tsp. allspice
1 tsp. powdered
  cloves

1 tsp. nutmeg
1 cup honey
1 cup strong coffee,
  cooled
¾ cup vegetable oil
1 tsp. vanilla
3 eggs
½ cup raisins
½ cup chopped
  walnuts

Preheat oven to 350°. Grease 12" tube pan. Sift all dry ingredients into a large bowl. Make a well and add all liquid ingredients. Mix together thoroughly. Add raisins and nuts. Pour into prepared pan.

Bake 50–60 minutes. Turn pan upside down. Cool cake completely before removing from pan.

12 servings

Yom Kippur Break-fast (Dairy)

Fruit Juice
*Zucchini Bisque
*Asparagus with
  Yogurt Sauce
*Herring Salad
  Smoked Fish
  Tuna Salad
  Cheeses

*Dairy Noodle Pudding *or*
*French Toast Casserole
  Breads and Bagels
  Salads
*Rugelach
  Cheese Cake
  Cookies

*recipe included

58

Zucchini Bisque

Do not allow ingredients to come to a boil during preparation or reheating.

1 Tbsp. olive oil
1 cup chopped leeks, white part only
2–3 cloves garlic, minced
3 small zucchini, coarsely chopped, not peeled

1 medium boiling potato, diced, not peeled
3 cups low-fat milk
salt and freshly ground black pepper, to taste

Heat olive oil in a large, heavy saucepan. Add leeks, garlic and zucchini. Cook over low heat, stirring occasionally, until all are tender but not brown—approximately 20 minutes.

Add potato and 2 cups of milk and simmer, covered, until the potato is tender—approximately 15 minutes. Puree contents of the saucepan in a blender or processor, and return to pan.

Add remaining 1 cup of milk, bring to a simmer, add salt and pepper to taste. May be served hot or cold.

4–6 servings

Asparagus in Yogurt Sauce

1 lb. fresh asparagus (thin stalks)
1 cup plain yogurt
¼ cup mayonnaise
⅓ cup dijon mustard
2 tsp. fresh, minced dill
1 Tbsp. fresh, minced chives
salt and freshly ground black pepper, to taste

Wash and remove bottoms of asparagus spears. Microwave or steam until just tender. Chill.

Combine remaining ingredients. Chill.

Just before serving, spoon some sauce over asparagus. Serve remaining sauce on the side.

Herring Salad

All ingredients should be <u>coarsely</u> chopped, not pureed.

1 jar herring snacks, 8 oz.
1 slice stale white bread
¼ cup cider vinegar
1 medium onion (purple, if available) cut in chunks

1 large stalk celery, sliced into 1" pieces
1 Granny Smith apple, peeled, cored, and quartered
1 hard boiled egg
1 Tbsp. sugar

Drain herring snacks and discard juice.

Soak bread in vinegar.

In food processor, process onion, celery and apple. Add egg, process for about 5 seconds. Add herring, bread, vinegar and sugar and process until coarsely chopped.

1½ cups

Dairy Noodle Pudding

1 lb. noodles, cooked and drained
1 lb. cottage cheese
½ pint sour cream
½ pint plain yogurt
1 cup milk

¼ lb. butter or margarine
½ cup sugar
4 eggs, lightly beaten
½ cup raisins
½ cup crushed pineapple, drained

Topping:

1 cup crushed corn flakes
1 tsp. cinnamon

¼ cup light brown sugar

Preheat oven to 350° (325° for glass pan). Grease 9" × 13" pan.

Combine noodles, cottage cheese, sour cream, yogurt, milk, butter or margarine, sugar, eggs, raisins and pineapple. Pour into prepared pan.

Combine topping ingredients. Sprinkle over pudding.

Bake for 35–45 minutes, until top is browned.

This recipe may be assembled one day ahead. If possible, remove from refrigerator an hour before baking.

12 servings

French Toast Casserole

1 10 oz. long, thin French or Italian bread, without seeds	3 tsp. sugar
	¾ tsp. salt
	1 Tbsp. vanilla
8 eggs	2 Tbsp. butter or
3 cups milk	margarine

Grease 9" × 13" pan. Cut bread into thick equal slices and arrange in one layer on bottom of pan. Except for butter, beat eggs with remaining ingredients. Pour over bread in pan. Cover with foil and refrigerate at least 4 hours, up to 36 hours. Uncover. Dot mixture with butter.

Place pan in cold oven. Bake at 350° (325° for glass pan) 45–50 minutes until bread is puffed and lightly brown. Let stand 5 minutes.

12 servings

Rugelach

½ lb. unsalted butter
½ lb. cream cheese
2 cups flour
2 tsp. cinnamon

2 Tbsp. sugar
½ cup finely ground nuts
½ cup raisins (optional)

Combine butter, cheese and flour. Mix well. Form into 4 equal pieces and refrigerate overnight, covered well.

Preheat oven to 375°. Grease a cookie sheet.

Roll out each piece of dough into a ⅛" thick circle. Sprinkle with cinnamon, sugar, nuts, and if desired, raisins.

Cut each round into 12 wedges. Roll up each wedge, starting at the wide edge. Turn corners to make a crescent and place on cookie sheet, seam side down.

Bake about 25 minutes. Remove from pan immediately and cool on racks.

4 dozen

Rosh HaShanah and Yom Kippur Study Questions

These questions and their answers are designed to initiate discussion and to encourage further study.

The Prague Mahzor. 1525. The Jewish Theological Seminary of America

Rosh HaShanah

1. How many New Years are on the Jewish calendar?

2. What is the significance of visiting graves during this period?

3. How is the observance of *Rosh HaShanah* different from new year celebrations of other peoples?

4. What is the relationship between the *Torah* and *Haftarah* readings?

5. Why do we blow the *shofar*? When is it blown? How many blasts are there in all?

6. What is the ten day cycle between *Rosh HaShanah* and *Yom Kippur* called?

7. What is the significance of the number 10 in Judaism?

8. Why can the first day of *Rosh HaShanah* never fall on a Sunday, Wednesday, or Friday?

9. Why are *ḥallot* usually baked in different shapes for this holiday?

10. Why do we dip apples in honey?

ANSWERS

1. There are four New Years on the Jewish calendar:

(a) 1st of *Nisan*—New Year for kings and festivals;

(b) 1st of *Elul*—New Year for the tithe of cattle;

(c) 1st of *Tishri*—reckoning of the years and jubilee years for planting and vegetables;

(d) 15th of *Shvat*—New Year of the Trees.

2. It is customary to visit the graves of dear ones *(kever avot)* in this penitential period, because remembering them invokes a mood of humility.

3. These are profoundly serious days, when moral inventories are taken. We are held accountable for our actions of the past year, and we promise ourselves that we will try to do better in the year to come.

4. The *Torah* reading on the first day retells the story of the birth of Isaac. Both Sarah and Rebekah had been childless and had prayed to God. On *Rosh HaShanah* their prayers were answered and subsequently they conceived and gave birth. The birth of Samuel is recorded in the *Haftarah*, for he too was born on *Rosh HaShanah*. On the second day, the *Torah* reading is of the binding of Isaac and the eventual sacrifice of a ram in his stead. The *Haftarah* from Jeremiah stresses the themes of God remembering the Jewish people and their return to Israel.

5. There are many explanations of why the *shofar* is blown. The sound of the *shofar* is analogous to the trumpet blasts which announce the coronation of a king. *Rosh HaShanah* is the birthday of the world and God is its sovereign. By sounding the *shofar* we acknowledge Him as our King. Also, it stirs our consciences, inducing us to confront our past errors and return to God. The *shofar* is blown on every morning of the month of *Elul*, except on *Shabbat*. It is blown on both days of *Rosh HaShanah*, except on *Shabbat*, as well as at

the end of the *N'ilah* service on *Yom Kippur.* It has been called a "prayer without words." It is a call to repentance and spiritual renewal. A total of 100 notes are traditionally blown on each day of *Rosh HaShanah.*

6. The period from *Rosh HaShanah* to *Yom Kippur* is called the "Ten Days of Repentance."

7. The days from *Rosh HaShanah* through *Yom Kippur* number 10; a quorum for Jewish religious worship is 10 (*minyan*); there are Ten Commandments; and, confessions of sins are recited 10 times on *Yom Kippur.*

8. The first day of *Rosh HaShanah* cannot be on a Wednesday or Friday so that *Yom Kippur* will neither be preceded nor followed by a *Shabbat*, which would entail having two con-secutive days on which it is forbidden to prepare food and bury the dead. If *Rosh HaShanah* fell on Sunday, *Hoshanah Rabbah* would occur on a *Shabbat* and we would not be able to circle the synagogue with a *lulav* and *etrog.*

9. The different shapes of *ḥallot* have different meanings: a ladder—God judges those who will descend and ascend; and, the most popular, the round loaf—suggesting a desire for a complete and long span of life.

10. Dipping fruit in honey is symbolic of our wish for a good and sweet year to come.

Yom Kippur

1. What does *Yom Kippur* mean?

2. Why do we fast?

3. Is *Yom Kippur* a day of sadness?

4. Why are confessional prayers written in the plural?

5. What does *Kol Nidre* mean? Why is it said three times?

6. Why are the confessional prayers written in alphabetical order?

7. Name the different services.

8. What is the significance of the *N'ilah service?*

Kiddush Cup.
S. Resnick,
New York, 1990.
Crystal, carved.
In The Spirit
Gallery

9. Why should we be especially sensitive to giving *tz'dakah* at this time of the year?

10. What is the significance of the *Haftarah* recited during *Minḥah* on *Yom Kippur?*

11. Why are *Torah* covers, ark curtains, and reading table covers white at this season?

12. Why do the rabbi and *ḥazzan*, as well as other members of the congregation, prostrate themselves during certain parts of the service?

ANSWERS

1. *Yom Kippur* means "Day of Atonement."

2. On this holiest of days, we remove ourselves from the petty clamors of mundane thoughts and actions. This is a day of physical abstinence. It is forbidden to eat, drink or partake of other physical pleasures. It is natural that repentance be preceded by an attempt at self-discipline.

3. Although not a joyous holiday, *Yom Kippur* should not be considered a day of sadness either. The central theme of atonement and reconciliation provides a mood of solemnity and holiness.

4. The confessional prayers are written in the plural in order to recognize how deeply we are involved in one another's weaknesses and failures, and to reinforce a sense of community.

5. *Kol Nidre* means "All Vows." It is chanted before the evening service of *Yom Kippur.* It is written as a legal document calling for the annulment of certain vows. A requirement for such a document was that it be recited three times. In order to be understood by the community-at-large, it was written in the vernacular—Aramaic.

6. Many of the prayers in Jewish liturgy are written in alphabetical order, or as acrostics, to make them easier to remember.

7. The different services of *Yom Kippur are: Ma'ariv* (evening), *Shaḥarit* (morning), *Musaf* (additional), *Minḥah* (afternoon), and *N'ilah* (closing).

8. The *N'ilah* is the final service of the long day, and the symbolic time of the "closing of the gates" of heaven to our prayers.

9. *Tz'dakah,* a cornerstone of Judaism, is more than the giving of money. It is, in reality, righteous or just conduct by one human being towards another, for the root word *"tzedek"* means "justice." In the High Holiday liturgy,

tz'dakah is one of the ways in which we may influence our future for good.

10. The *Haftarah* for *Yom Kippur* afternoon is the Book of Jonah read in its entirety. It illustrates the power of repentance and shows that man cannot escape the presence of God.

11. White is the traditional color for the Days of Awe, symbolizing purity. Many people also wear white clothing.

12. In the ritual of the Temple, the *Kohanim* (Priests) and the people prostrated themselves, and this is described during the *Avodah* service of *Yom Kippur.*

Glossary

Aseret Y'may T'shuvah: the Ten Days of Repentance from *Rosh HaShanah* until the end of *Yom Kippur.*

Avodah: the part of the *Musaf* or additional service for *Yom Kippur* describing specific rites in the Temple in Jerusalem.

Birkat HaMazon: blessings recited after meals.

B'rakhah (b'rakhot): formula(s) for acknowledging God's sovereignty; blessing.

Deuteronomy: fifth book of the Bible, *D'varim* in Hebrew.

Elul: last month of the Jewish year, preceding *Rosh HaShanah.*

Genesis: first book of the Bible, *B'rayshit* in Hebrew.

Usque Maḥzor. Ferrara, 1553. The Jewish Theological Seminary of America

G'mar Hatimah Tovah/ G'mar Tov: "May the sealing end well"/"A good ending," the greeting offered between *Rosh HaShanah* and *Yom Kippur.*

Haftarah: selection from a book of the Prophets (*N'vi'im* in Hebrew) read after the Torah reading on *Shabbat* and Festivals.

Hallah (Hallot): the special bread(s) eaten on *Shabbat* and Festivals.

Havdalah: literally "separation;" the ceremony at the conclusion of *Shabbat* or a Festival separating it from the rest of the week.

Hazzan: cantor.

Holy of Holies: most sacred chamber of the Temple in Jerusalem, entered only once a year by the *Kohen Gadol.*

Hoshana Rabba: the seventh day of the Festival of *Sukkot.*

Kiddush: the *b'rakhah* over wine recited on *Shabbat,* Festivals, and special occasions.

Kohen Gadol: the "high priest," who was a descendant of Aaron.

Kol Nidre: "All vows," the opening words of the service on the eve of *Yom Kippur.*

K'tivah v'Hatimah Tovah: "May you be inscribed and sealed for a good (year)," greeting offered between *Rosh HaShanah* and *Yom Kippur.*

Levites: descendants of the tribe of Levi who had specific ritual obligations and responsibilities in the Temple.

Leviticus: third book of the Bible, *Va'yikra* in Hebrew.

L'Shanah Tovah T'katayvu: "May you be written for a good year," a greeting offered during the High Holiday season.

Ma'ariv: the evening service.

Mahzor: literally "Cycle," the book containing the services for Festivals and the High Holy days.

Malkhuyot: segment of *Rosh HaShanah Musaf* service.

Martyrology: section of *Yom Kippur Musaf* service relating the deaths of ten Jewish leaders during the Roman persecution. Also called *ayleh ezk'rah* "These I remember. . ." from its first words in Hebrew.

Midrash: homiletical parables and/or anecdotes; rabbinic expounding on text.

Minhah: the afternoon service.

Mishnah: the expansion of Biblical legislation committed to writing about 200 C.E.; the basis of the *Talmud.*

Mishneh Torah: Code of Jewish Law written by Maimonides.

Mitzvah: a commandment.

Motzi: abbreviated name for the *b'rakhah* recited before eating bread; by extension, the *b'rakhah* recited before meals.

Musaf: the additional section of the morning service for *Shabbat,* Festivals and *Rosh Hodesh.*

N'ilat Sh'arim: "Closing of the Gates", the closing service for *Yom Kippur.*

Numbers: fourth book of the Bible, *B'midbar* in Hebrew.

Pilgrimage Festivals: Pesah, Shavuot, Sukkot, the occasions on which Israelites traveled to the Temple in Jerusalem.

Piyyut(im): liturgical poem(s).

Rosh HaShanah: the New Year.

Rosh Hodesh: the beginning of a new month.

Sephardim: Jews of Spanish-Portuguese and Oriental descent.

Shabbat: the seventh day, Sabbath.

Shabbat Shuvah: Sabbath of Return, between *Rosh HaShanah* and *Yom Kippur.*

Shaḥarit: the morning service.

Shanah Tovah (um'tukah): "a good (and sweet) year," a greeting offered during the High Holiday season.

Shehehe'yanu: ". . .Who has kept us alive," the key word in the *b'rakhah* said on special occasions, or the first time something is done.

Sh'ma: the first word of several passages from the Bible which are recited mornings and evenings. The opening verse is: "Hear, O Israel: the Lord is our God, the Lord is One."

Shmini Atzeret: the Eighth Day of Assembly which falls immediately after *Sukkot.*

Shofar: the ram's horn, sounded, except on *Shabbat,* on the High Holidays and on each morning of *Elul.*

Shofarot: a segment of the *Rosh HaShanah Musaf* service.

Sh'varim: three short blasts of the *shofar.*

Simḥat Torah: the second day of the holiday of *Shmini Atzeret* when the public reading of the last section of the *Torah* is completed, and the first lines of Genesis are begun.

S'liḥot: special penitential prayers recited before *Rosh HaShanah* and during the *Yom Kippur* service.

Sukkah: the temporary booth erected for use during the Festival of *Sukkot.*

Sukkot: the Festival of Tabernacles or Booths.

Talmud: the body of post-Biblical Jewish law and tradition recorded in the *Mishnah* and *G'mara.*

Tashlikh: custom on *Rosh HaShanah* to symbolically "cast sins into the water."

T'fillah (t'fillot): prayer(s).

Tishri: the first month of the Jewish year, in which *Rosh HaShanah* falls.

T'kiah: unbroken *shofar* note.

T'kiah G'dolah: the great blast of the *shofar,* held as long as possible.

Torah: the first five books of the Bible.

T'ruah: shofar call of nine staccato blasts.

T'shuvah: return, repentance.

Tz'dakah: just and proper action, frequently translated as "charity."

Torah Shield. Germany, ca. 1690. Silver, embossed. The Jewish Museum

Tzom Kal: "a light, or easy, fast," a greeting for *Yom Kippur.*

Yamim Nora'im: Rosh HaShanah and *Yom Kippur.*

Yahrzeit: (Yiddish) annual commemoration of the date of death.

Yizkor: memorial prayers recited on *Yom Kippur* and Festivals.

Yom HaDin: Day of Judgment.

Yom HaZikaron: Day of Remembrance.

79

Yom Kippur: Day of Atonement.

Yom T'ruah: Day of Blowing the Horn.

Yom Tzom: fast day.

Zikhronot: segment of *Rosh HaShanah Musaf* service.

Bibliography

Arzt, Max, <u>Justice and Mercy,</u> (New York: Burning Bush Press, 1963). (Out of print)

Birnbaum, Philip, <u>A Book of Jewish Concepts,</u> (New York: Hebrew Publishing Company, 1964).

Eisenstein, Judith Kaplan, <u>Heritage of Music,</u> The Music of the Jewish People, (New York: Union of American Hebrew Congregations, 1969).

Goodman, Philip, <u>The Rosh Hashanah Anthology,</u> (Philadelphia: The Jewish Publication Society of America, 1970).

, <u>The Yom Kippur Anthology,</u> (Philadelphia: The Jewish Publication Society of America, 1971).

, <u>Rejoice in Thy Festival,</u> (New York: Bloch Publishing Co., 1956).

Greenberg, Sidney and Jonathan D. Levine, eds., <u>Mahzor Hadash,</u> (Bridgeport, Connecticut: The Prayer Book Press of Media Judaica, 1977).

Torah Finials.
Ludwig Wolpert,
New York, NY,
1963. Silver. The
Jewish Museum

Harlow, Jules, ed., Maḥzor for Rosh Hashanah and Yom Kippur, (New York: The Rabbinical Assembly, 1972).

Klein, Isaac, A Guide to Jewish Religious Practice, (New York: The Jewish Theological Seminary of America, 1979).

Schauss, Hayyim, The Jewish Festivals, (New York: Union of American Hebrew Congregations, 1938).

Siegel, Richard, Strassfeld, Michael, Strassfeld, Sharon, The Jewish Catalog, (Philadelphia: The Jewish Publication Society of America, 1973).

Silverman, Morris, High Holiday Prayer Book (Hartford, Connecticut: Prayer Book Press, 1951).

Strassfeld, Michael, The Jewish Holidays, (New York: Harper & Row Publishers, 1985).

Trepp, Leo, The Complete Book of Jewish Observance, (New York: Behrman House, 1980).

Encyclopedia Judaica, (Jerusalem: Keter Publishing House, 1972).

For Children

Abrams, Judith Z., <u>Rosh Hashanah Service,</u> (Rockville, MD: Kar-Ben Copies, 1990).

, <u>Yom Kippur Serivce,</u> (Rockville, MD: Kar-Ben Copies, 1990).

, <u>Selichot Services,</u> (Rockville, MD: Kar-Ben Copies,1990).

Cohen, Barbara, <u>Even Higher,</u> (New York: Lothrop, Lee & Shepard Books,). Illustrated by Anatoly Ivanov.

Simon, Norma, <u>Rosh Hashanah,</u> (New York: United Synagogue).

, <u>Yom Kippur,</u> (New York: United Synagogue).

Singer, Marilyn, <u>Minnie's Yom Kippur Birthday,</u> (New York, Harper & Row). Illustrated by Ruth Rosner.

<u>The Wizard of Av: Rosh Hashana Book & Calendar</u> (New York: Shapolsky Publishers).

For the Entire Family

Together: A Child-Parent Kit (New York: Melton Research Center of the Jewish Theological Seminary of America, 1984).

NOTES

NOTES

NOTES

NOTES

NOTES

NOTES

NOTES

NOTES